MY BRAIN, MY BRAIN, MY BEAUTIFUL BRAIN

SHAWN T. LETFORD,
GENEIN M. LETFORD, M.ED
Illustrated by SHAYNE LETFORD & BRIEFSTOCK

Thank you Joy 'Nana' Letford and Denzil 'Grandpa' Letford for helping me grow my creative brain. -STL

This book is dedicated to Dr. Marian Diamond, one of the founders of modern neuroscience and a pioneer of the idea that the brain continues to change throughout life. Though she faced opposition and discrimination with presenting this new discovery, she was persistent and bold. Dr. Diamond loved the brain, as do I, and it is an honor to create books and teachings based on her work. -GML

...

Additional Character Illustrations by Briefstock
Poetry Editor: Meeg Pincus

Library of Congress Cataloging-in-Publication Data is available upon request.

Paperback ISBN 979-8-9885237-0-3
eBook ISBN 979-8-9885237-1-0

Forward

The creative mind is a gift that is available to every child. So why is it that some children appear to be extremely creative and others less so? Could it have something to do with how children 'see' themselves in their world? How do they show up in their daily lives? From the point of view of Learning Sciences that are informed by cognitive neuroscience, every child is an explicit example of 'differential neurobiological susceptibility to social context'.

Every brain is unique; every brain is hardwired to be who we are. When people learn they can change their thoughts, actions, and beliefs, it then is possible to adjust our neurobiological (hardwired) sensitivity to manage situations, people, and places. This knowledge is a creative gift that children and adults can attain.

In this creative collection, "*My Brain, My Brain, My Beautiful Brain*", elements of foundational neuroscience are expressed in short clear adventuresome couplets and connected to novel and useful concepts that illuminate the working brain.

Since the 'decade of the brain' at the turn of this century, troves of new information have become available to scientists, parents, leaders, and teachers. In addition, meaningful elements of brain structure and brain function have made their way into the workforce and children's learning spaces as they also begin to ingest mental models, new vocabulary, and contextual processes that are both elegant and complex. We are all being introduced to our brain in a whole new way.

The cognitive creative space is today's clear winner. We are aware of the internal potential, the limitless exponential growth that is available to each and every one of us. The journey begins with awareness and vocabulary. It amplifies with mental models and fun. It ends with creativity. Take this exciting book along on your learning journey.

Timothy Kieran O'Mahony, Ph.D., FRGS,
Cognitive Neuroscientist
Founder, The Institute for Connecting Neuroscience
With Teaching and Learning in Seattle, WA.

My brain, my brain
My beautiful brain,
Ideas flow through it
Like rivers of rain.

My brain is a wonder
Helps me do all I do,
As I live and create
And the same goes for you!

My brain has six sections
Combining like art,
To allow me to function—
I'll show you, let's start!

Like the stem of a flower
This part keeps me alive—
From my heartbeat to breathing,
What I need to survive!

CEREBELLUM

When I walk, run or dance
Or I skate 'round a rink,
This part aids in movement,
Helps me balance and to THINK!

This part helps me name
All the things that I see,
Such as colors and shapes
Like the ones of this tree!

OCCIPITAL LOBE

PARIETAL LOBE

All five of my senses
Are helped by this part,
So I see, hear, and feel things
Like this piece of art!

SAD
BORED
CURIOUS
ELATED

These two lobes are like twins
Helping me understand,
All your words and your feelings
And remember our plans!

FRONTAL LOBE

When I've got a tough problem
Really making me think,
This big part saves the day
Letting my ideas link!

My brain, my brain
My marvelous brain,
It allows me to soar
Like a beautiful crane.

Knowing how its parts work
Helps me understand why
My brain keeps me growing,
Past the limits of the sky.

All its parts work together
Helping me to be smart
In eight ways that we know of—
I'll show you, let's start!

So much great information
Is found in the trees,
Nature's systems and ways
Spark my mind like the breeze.

When I twist, turn and flip,
Objects move in my mind,
So I balance and know
What's ahead and behind.

SPATIAL

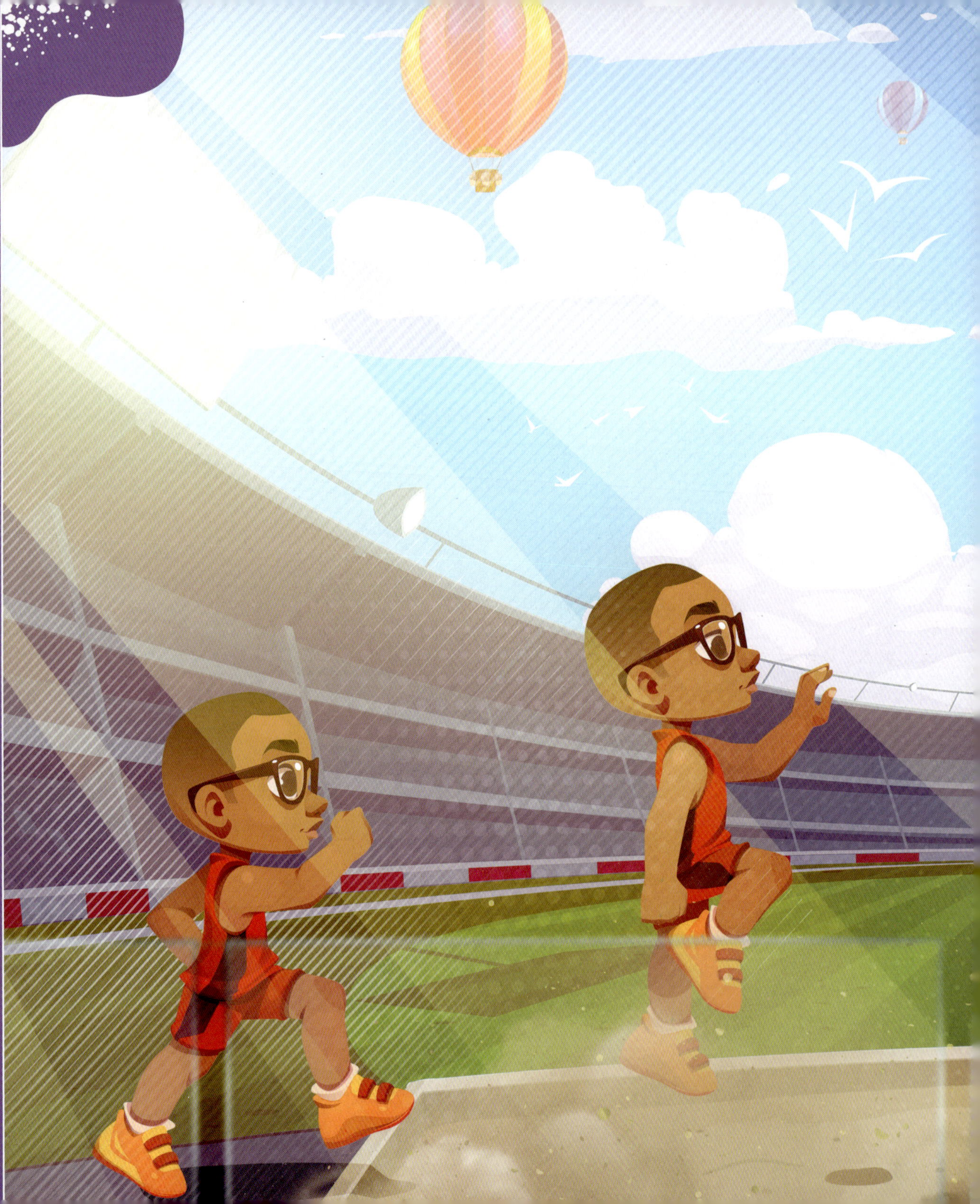

Running, skiing, or playing
I can coordinate
With my mind and my movements
Whether bending or straight!

When I'm faced with a puzzle
Or a question in math,
I can come up with answers
Using logic's clear path.

shoes

I Have an
IDEA!

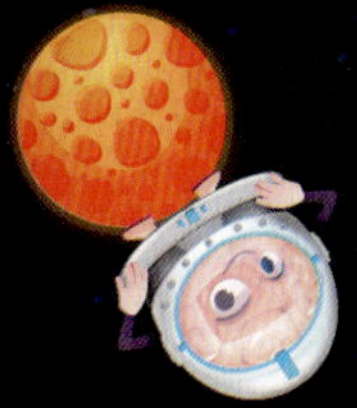

If I need the right words
To explain my creations,
I tap into language,
And connect across nations.

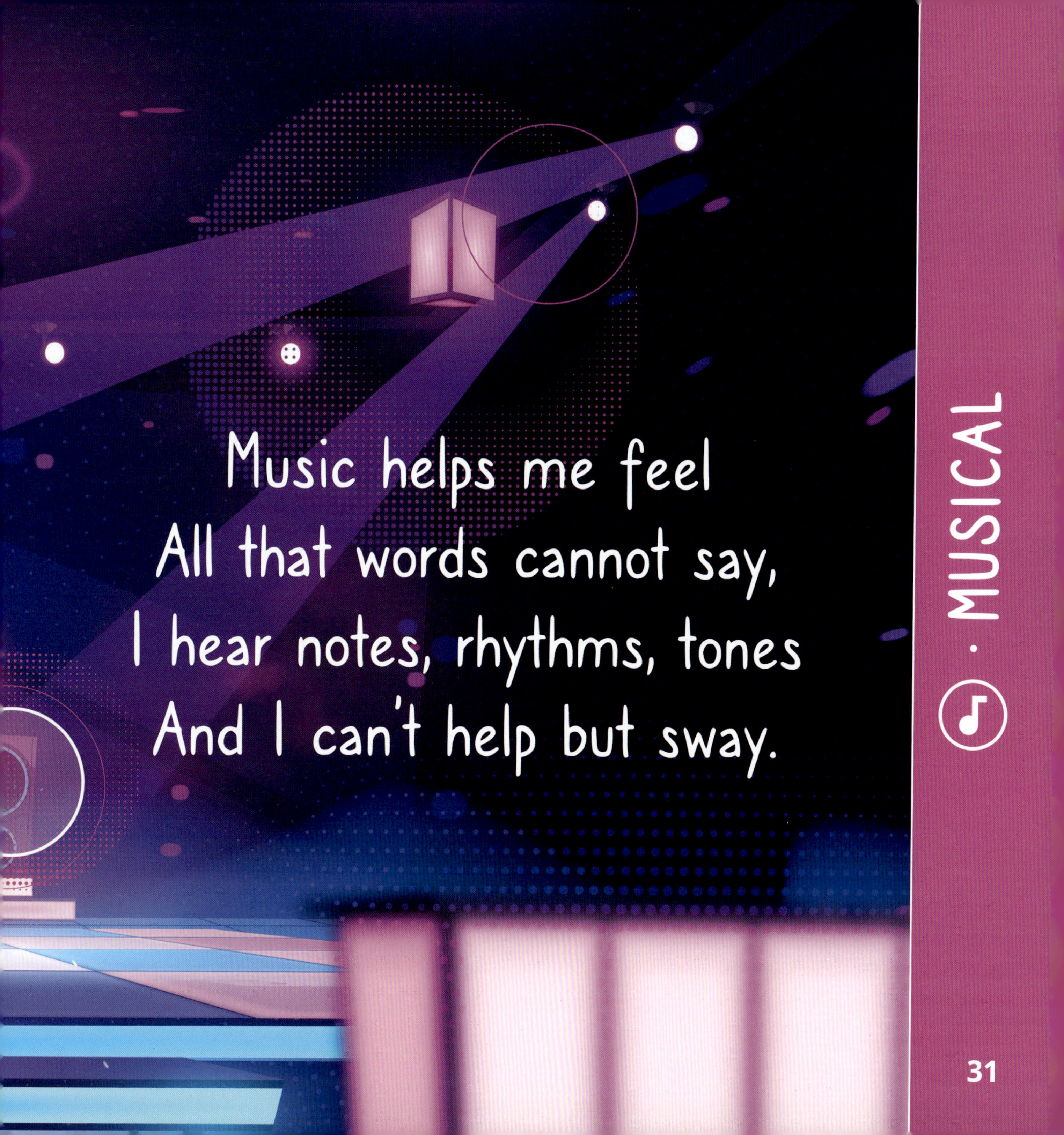

Music helps me feel
All that words cannot say,
I hear notes, rhythms, tones
And I can't help but sway.

Creating connections
With people I meet
Comes from sensing their feelings
And finding their beat.

INTERPERSONAL

INTRAPERSONAL

Pondering my own choices,
My own reasons and strengths,
Helps me to lead
And grow to great lengths.

My brain, my brain
My wonderful brain,
It moves me through life
Like a powerful train.

It allows me to function
Using all its six parts,
And it helps me create things
With eight kinds of smarts.

Every day I can thank it
For all that I do,
And for helping connect me
To new friends like...
you!

Dear Parents, Teachers, Leaders, and Caregivers,

Our brains are magnificent. The creative potential they hold is larger than the universe. Even though your adult brain is only a 3-pound tofu-like complex organ, it is responsible for your thoughts, memory, emotions, touch, motor skills, vision, breathing, and every process that regulates your body!

And your creativity!

With the advancement of fMRI technology and now, the more transportable fNIRS technology, we can better understand what our brains are doing inside our own heads and while in concert with other brains. Our family, the founders of Intercultural Creativity® and NeuroSomatic Creativity®, believes that creativity and social, emotional, and academic intelligence can improve when we know, understand, and utilize our brains to the best of our ability.

My Brain, My Brain, My Beautiful Brain looks like a children's book, but we call our children's books 'Inner Child' books because our books are meant for adults as well as children. Our 'Inner Child' books are for anyone who needs to discover, or rediscover, new elements of themselves and see the possibility of their creative minds within their social and cultural environments.

Let's jump into a deep dive of *My Brain, My Brain, My Beautiful Brain*.

SECTION ONE

Your brain and your child's brain have MANY parts (such as the amygdala, hippocampus, striatum, and corpus callosum to name a few) but in this first literary project, we'll only focus on the six main sections. Our future books will dive into other areas and functions of our awesome integrated brain and its many networks. Here are the main six sections:

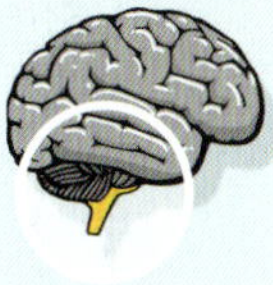
page 6

Brain Stem:

Automation! Automation! Automation! Functions of the brain stem regulate many bodily activities, including heart rhythm, breathing, blood flow, and oxygen and carbon dioxide levels. The medulla, which is in the brain stem, produces reflexive activities such as vomiting, coughing, swallowing, and sneezing. Achoo! Shawn often says, "Thank you brain stem for keeping me alive and doing all the things I need you to do without my instructions!"

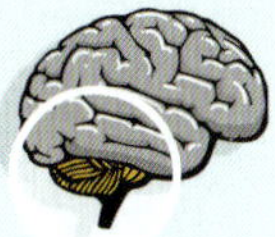
page 8

Cerebellum:

Neuroscientists call the cerebellum your 'little brain' because it's packed with so many neurons. The primary function of the cerebellum is to help you maintain balance, posture, and equilibrium. It's activated when you voluntarily move, walk, dance, and are physically active.

Karate or Zumba anyone?

Recently, neuroscientists have found that the cerebellum not only helps keep you upright and balanced, but it also monitors your prefrontal cortex, the part of the brain that helps you think, make decisions and plan for the future.

So, what does this mean?

This means movement, dance and other types of physical activity help you think more efficiently in all types of creativity. When Shawn is dancing, I remind him that he is using his cerebellum and helping his brain integrate experiences and think more clearly in order to combine new ideas.

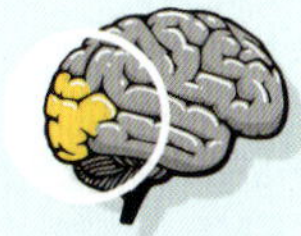
page 10

Occipital Lobe:

Do you see what I see? The occipital lobe is in the back part of the brain and is involved with vision.

But here's one thing you probably did not know.

Your previous experiences greatly influence what you are currently seeing. Information collected from the eyes goes through the thalamus (the gatekeeper for most of the senses) before heading to the occipital lobe. Even though there is a lot of information going from the eyes through the thalamus to the occipital lobe, there is SIX TIMES as much information going in the *opposite* direction, from the brain's occipital lobe to the thalamus back to the eyes.

Therefore, the things you *think* you are seeing are heavily influenced by your previous beliefs, expectations, and even your biases. This is why having diverse experiences, seeing things from multiple perspectives, being curious, and pausing on snap judgments are important for growing your self-awareness and Intercultural Creativity®. Shawn continuously observes with intention and looks for visual connections to develop his ability to 'see beyond the obvious' in his environment.

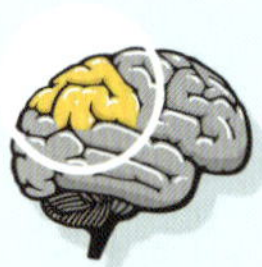

page 12

Parietal Lobe:

Hanging out in the middle part of the brain, the parietal lobe is a major interpreter of the sensory world around your body. It helps you identify objects and understand spatial relationships (where your body is compared with objects around you). The parietal lobe is also involved in interpreting pain and touch in the body. As a parent, educator, and corporate facilitator, I incorporate many sensory touch points into my lessons in order to activate and involve the parietal lobe. This lobe also houses Wernicke's area, which helps the brain understand spoken language.

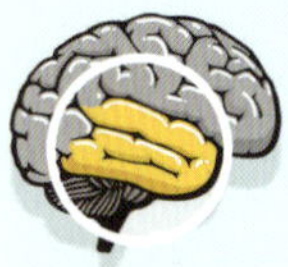

page 14

Temporal Lobes:

Located at the sides of the brain, the temporal lobes are involved in short-term memory, speech, musical rhythm, and some degree of smell recognition. The temporal lobes sit behind the ears and are the second largest lobe. They are most commonly associated with processing auditory information and with the encoding of memory. The temporal lobes are also believed to play an important role in processing emotions, language, and certain aspects of visual perception.

The dominant temporal lobe, which is the left side in most people, is involved in understanding language and learning and remembering verbal information. The non-dominant lobe, which is typically the right temporal lobe, is involved in learning and remembering non-verbal information (e.g. visual-spatial material and music). This is probably one reason why it is easier to recall concepts put to music! Shawn and his father compose songs about everything, even asparaGUS! Remember how you learned your ABCs? Please keep singing!

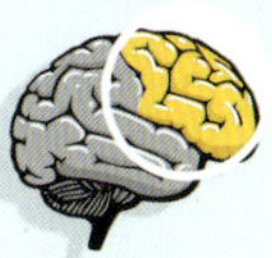
page 16

The Frontal Lobe:

Attention! Attention! I would like to introduce you to your brain's executive team. This is the part of your brain that maintains 'executive control' and attention. The frontal lobe is located directly behind the forehead and is the most susceptible to head injury. Let's protect it at all costs! The frontal lobe is important for voluntary movement, expressive language, and, as in the introduction, for managing higher-level executive functions.

Executive functions refer to a collection of cognitive (thinking) and creative skills including the capacity to plan, organize, initiate, imagine, self-monitor, and control one's responses in order to achieve a goal. The frontal lobe is considered our behavior and emotional control center and home to our personality. It plays a major role in what makes you … you.

If you and your child understand and get control of this area, you both will be in better control of your lives and how you respond to events that are out of your control. People who practice improvisation also learned how to quiet this area down so unusual creative ideas can surface into conscious thought.

Shawn uses two main strategies to get his executive center back online in high-stress situations; breathing and symbolic labeling, which is naming the emotion and sharing why he is having that feeling. This strategy, coupled with breathing, helps us all have a clearer picture of the event, perspective shift to someone else's point of view, and create an action response plan to the situation. Breathe in and breathe out.

SECTION TWO

Celebrating Our Multiple Intelligences

Now that we have met some of the key players in our cerebral journey, let's see how they perform in an integrated, dynamic way when they are stimulated creatively. In 1983, Malcolm Gardner addressed the concern that the only type of intelligence our schools and society acknowledged was academic and logical intelligence. This type of intelligence was mostly determined through various standardized tests such as the IQ test, SAT or ACT. There was no celebration, or even acknowledgment, of other types of 'smarts', such as emotional, kinesthetic, musical, or social intelligence, to name a few.

He, and other concerned psychologists such as Daniel Goleman, began to publish findings to claim there are several other ways the brain can impressively collect, integrate and apply knowledge to the outside world and in various social situations for personal and professional success. Gardner called these the 'Eight Multiple Intelligences'. Even though the literature is always evolving and advancing, we believe there are more than eight (such as creative intelligence). Our family chose to share these eight as an initial framework, communicating that someone can be 'smart' in more ways than one and in many ways simultaneously.

The Brain Evidence for Multiple Intelligences

Neuroscience evidence now reveals a neural bridge between IQ-type academic skills and these eight intelligences. Each of the multiple intelligences can serve as a 'delivery route' to support important cognitive and emotional processes that are needed for learning, such

as attention, memory, motivation, creative cognition, problem-solving, and understanding. For those who love definitions, here is one for intelligence:

"Intelligence is a biopsychological potential to process information that can be activated in a cultural setting to solve problems or create products that are of value in a culture."

That's an academic way to say intelligence, especially when it is coupled with wisdom, is the ability to gain and integrate knowledge and use it with people from diverse backgrounds in various situations.

Here's an even simpler way:
You know a lot of stuff and can use that information to help many types of people in all types of ways!

So, what are these foundational eight intelligences? Shawn already introduced them to you in the book. Here are the explanations, the core cognitive units and the brain regions each intelligence uses. If it says, 'Subcortical Regions' this includes the corpus callosum, hippocampus, amygdala, thalamus, and putamen regions. Oh, what fun!

NATURALISTIC INTELLIGENCE

page 20

Being creative involves being observant of the obvious and mundane information around us. One of the best ways to be in awe and discover creative operations is to observe nature, animals, and natural systems. Messages are in the mundane. Wisdom is hidden in the ordinary.

Allowing our children, and our adults, to explore their natural surroundings with a curious, investigative eye will spark their own creative thinking in all areas. Nature teaches us that one cannot survive without a relationship. Being observant of relationships, cause and effect, cycles, and how natural objects and animals are built can inspire children and adults alike to create new combinations of ideas in their own world. Biomimicry is the process of humans inventing products and services inspired by objects, systems or animals found in nature.

There is a raft of research showing how being in nature, looking at the color of nature's green and even listening to songbirds has a positive effect on our mental and brain health. We are interconnected with nature. We are one.

So go outside and explore, look closely, ask questions, and find the miracle in the mundane all around you.

Core Cognitive Functions: Understanding Living Entities, Cause, and Effect, Metaphorical Relationships, Natural Systems, Understanding Animals and Plant Life, Unified Diversity

Brain Regions Used: Temporal, Subcortical Regions

SPATIAL INTELLIGENCE

page 22

Being able to rotate and manipulate objects in your imagination is an important creative, imaginative, and inventive thinking skill. Many psychologists see this task as a sign of high intelligence. One way to strengthen this skill is to give people (kids and adults alike) the opportunity to build things with their hands and rotate the concrete objects. Let them look at it from multiple perspectives. Let them identify what is visible and what is not visible. Let their imagination fill in the hidden spots. Rotate and look. Look and rotate.

You can also have people go outside and move their bodies throughout space. Interact with the objects around them, such as trees, fountains, and sculptures.

Create visual art. In their drawings or observations of the artwork, point out and dialogue about the use of positive (filled) and negative (empty) space. By manipulating objects in space within their tangible reality, they will better

create, imagine and manipulate spatial concepts in their mind.
Core Cognitive Functions: Spatial Cognition, Working With Objects, Visual Arts, Spatial Navigation.

Brain Regions Used: Frontal, Parietal, Temporal, Occipital Lobes

KINESTHETIC INTELLIGENCE

page 24

Do you like to MOVE IT, MOVE IT? Well, you should. Here's why.

Movement from infancy into adulthood is critical for brain growth and brain wiring. Even the developmental act of a baby crawling strengthens both hemispheres of the brain and the corpus callosum (the part that connects both hemispheres and helps get information back and forth between hemispheres). Being intentional with movement from day one is essential.

Your body is an instrument of thought. The relationship between the body and the mind is now recognized by neuroscientists as being bi-directional and parallel, rather than just the mind directing the body. It's a two-way street. This is the foundational concept of our family's NeuroSomatic Creativity® framework and research. Embodied cognition is here to stay.

Allow people to do gross motor movements (using the whole body) and fine motor movements (using the fingers and toes) about the concepts they are learning in order to maximize memory and understanding. Since the cerebellum is heavily involved in movement and balance, moving helps you think more efficiently because the cerebellum also monitors the processes of the prefrontal cortex, where executive functions occur. Movement also helps build strong spatial cognition in people, which has been associated with increased skills in math, science, and technology.

Stuck on a problem? Get up and move!

Wish to think more creatively? Go take a dance class or skip down the street! Sing a song while you're at it!

We now have many more reasons why we like to MOVE IT, MOVE IT!

Core Cognitive Functions: Body Awareness, Body Control, Whole Body Movement, Dexterity, Symbolic Movement, Metaphorical Interpretation, Rhythm to Movement Associations, Embodied Cognition

Brain Regions Used: Subcortical, Cerebellum, Frontal, Parietal lobes

LOGICAL INTELLIGENCE

page 26

This type of intelligence is what most people think is the only type of intelligence.

Think about the problem. Memorize the steps of the formula to figure out the problem. Complete the problem. Get from Point A to Point B.

This type of thinking is important to have and needs to be developed. We all can practice how to think critically and analytically about a challenge.

Nevertheless, a non-linear type of thinking is important as well, especially in this new workforce, which is complex, ambiguous, and has no clear formula to get to the answer at the back of the book. In fact, there are no answers at the back of life's book!

Using our whole brain and ALL of these types of intelligences creatively will aid our children and adults in being adaptable in a non-linear world. So practice how to think logically but also give yourself nonlinear problems, so you can use your creative brain to create new neural paths!

Core Cognitive Functions for Logical: Logical Reasoning, Critical Thought, Convergent Thinking.

Brain Regions Used: Frontal, Parietal, Temporal lobes.

LINGUISTIC INTELLIGENCE

page 28

Communication is the flow of information and ideas from one brain to another. One way to do this is through the use of language. Words are powerful and can influence, create and shape the imagination of another human being. Being able to communicate your creative ideas through storytelling, the arts, and media is a skill that will become more and more valuable as our workforce shifts to a more creative workforce.

Additionally, if someone is multilingual, they are at an advantage, linguistically and neurologically speaking. Per the work of Dr. Nina Kraus, multilingual people have more gray matter in their brains and can think and manipulate concepts from more perspectives. She claims music and multilingualism are superpowers for brain development throughout life. It has large effects during the early stages of life and has been shown to slow the effects of hearing issues, dementia, and other neurodegenerative diseases in the late stages of life.

If possible, expose children to an additional language as early as possible. Singing songs and talking directly to someone who speaks that language are the quickest ways to become multilingual. If you are multilingual, celebrate it and continue to develop all of your languages. Languages are idea carriers and social connectors. The more diversity you have with your ability to communicate, the more people you can creatively connect with and create with.

Core Cognitive Functions: Speech, Reading, Writing, Multimodal Communication of Meaning, Conceptual Translation.

Brain Regions Used: Temporal, Frontal, and Parietal lobes

MUSICAL INTELLIGENCE

page 30

Music, as previously mentioned, is one of the brain's superpowers. Our family believes this to be true and even holds music and reading with the same status and importance. Producing music activates multiple sections of the brain at the same time. It strengthens the corpus callosum, allowing for more information to get back and forth between the hemispheres.

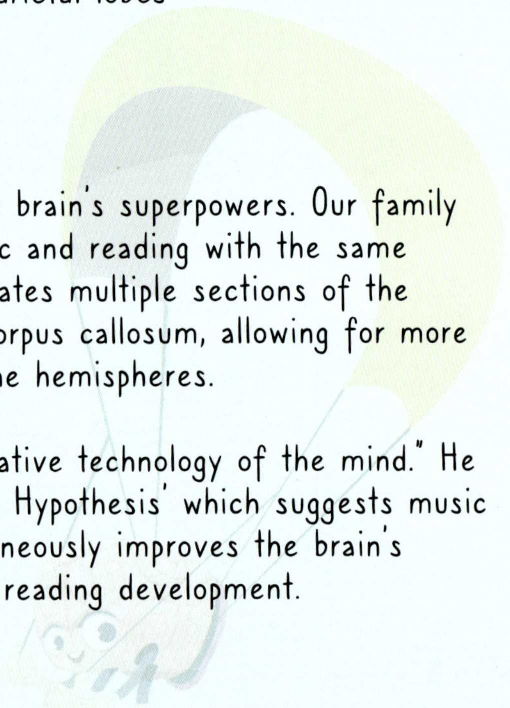

Dr. Ani Patel claims, "Music is the transformative technology of the mind." He offers a musical acronym called 'The OPERA Hypothesis' which suggests music training, especially in early childhood, simultaneously improves the brain's ability for phonic discrimination, speech, and reading development.

OPERA stands for the following:

O - **Overlap** = The brain networks involved in both speech and music overlap in the brain

P – **Precision** = Music places a higher demand on these networks than does speech (Did you play a C or a C sharp?)

E – **Emotion** = Musical activities that engage this network cause strong positive emotion

R – **Repetition** = Musical activities that engage this network are frequently repeated

A – **Attention** = Musical activities that engage this network are associated with focused attention

Both Doctors Ani Patel and Nina Kraus claim that children who learn music will have the additional benefit of a stronger speech and sound discrimination ability that will enhance their reading development in their early years and slow down the aging effects of hearing issues in their elderly years.

But it doesn't stop there.

Additionally, musicians tend to have higher emotional intelligence, a stronger working memory, higher sensitivity to patterns, greater ability to manipulate data in their auditory imagination, sensitivity to pitch in speech conversations and can translate ideas from one medium to another. Music is also connected to the movement networks in the brain. Maybe that's why we love to dance when the music turns on! I like to MOVE IT MOVE IT!

Core Cognitive Functions: Music Perception, Emotional Communication, Music Aesthetics and Production, Memory, Pattern Recognition

Brain Regions Used: Subcortical, Cerebellum, Frontal, Temporal Lobes

INTERPERSONAL INTELLIGENCE

page 32

Social intelligence is quickly moving forward to being one of the most important forms of intelligence. The work of my former UCLA professor, Dr. Matthew Lieberman, who is the author of the book '*Social: How Our Brains are Wired to Connect*', suggests that our brains are social brains by default. We are in fact WIRED to connect with one another. When we form relationships with people, especially with people with different lived experiences and cultures, our brains rewire our neural pathways due to these new interpersonal connections. Their stories become our stories and, on many occasions, their ideas can become our ideas. We learn how to tap into their 'Theory of Mind', which is the ability to perceive someone's thoughts, motivations, and desires and connect them to behavior. Understanding the theory of mind of others is a social skill that affects our ability to create new ideas and perspectives.

Encourage children and adults to add to their network of friends and increase the diversity of people in that network. Delay judgment when meeting new people. Share stories, share cultural similarities and differences, and be curious. Read, learn, and be open to the new adventures others can take you on by living and walking in their shoes.

Core Cognitive Functions: Social Perception, Interpersonal Understanding, Social Effectiveness, Leadership, Emotional Intelligence

Brain Regions Used: Cingulate, Parietal, Frontal, Temporal Lobes

INTRAPERSONAL INTELLIGENCE

page 34

Me, myself, and I.

Intrapersonal intelligence involves the capacity to understand oneself, to have an effective working model of oneself–including one's own desires, fears, and capacities–and to use such information effectively in regulating one's own life.

You will be more successful in regulating your own life when you understand the brain's role in this process. Now, when you cease focusing on the outside world and take the time to think to yourself and with yourself, what is actually happening in your brain?

A few decades ago, neuroscientists were doing task experiments with human subjects in an fMRI study. When the subject was just asked to lie there and do nothing, the scientists thought the screen that showed brain activity would quiet down. Strangely, when they looked at the screen, they saw low-frequency brain activity.

Wait?!? What?!?! They weren't expecting this at all!

This discovery, called the Default Mode Network (DMN), turned out to be one of the biggest neurological discoveries of the 21st century. Dr. Matthew Lieberman calls it your 'Social Brain' and claims that when turned on, it reviews your past, present and future social relationships and experiences. Dr. Michael Platt, the director of The Neuroscience Initiative at the Wharton School, calls it 'The Innovation Network' and believes it is when your brain is combining and recombining old ideas and information into new associations.

For me, it's a mixture of both. When my DMN is on, I think up new ideas, but I also review what happened yesterday at the work session I taught or what my husband commented about my meatloaf!

How do you turn this Default Mode Network on? Daydream. Take a shower. Go for a walk. Fold laundry. Stare out the window like Shawn. Think to yourself while doing undemanding work. Do things that don't need your full attention so your DMN can power on and start doing its 'invisible work', as Dr. Natalie Nixon calls it. Your Default Mode Network is often where your best ideas come from. Do the invisible work of wonder.

Core Cognitive Functions: Self Awareness, Self-Regulation, Executive Functions, Self-Other Management, Leadership, Imagination, Emotional Intelligence, Interoception

Brain Regions Used: Cingulate, Subcortical, Parietal, Frontal, Temporal lobes

Bringing It All Together: Synthesizing Your Intelligences

Integration is our goal. The brain needs integration. Our thinking needs integration. We need to integrate our experiences, our networks, and our creativity. Like myself, Dr. Gardner claims that he has a "synthesizing mind"— the ability to survey experiences and data across a wide range of disciplines and perspectives. The ability to celebrate and develop multiple intelligences will help our children be exemplary synthesizers. Gardner contends that the synthesizing mind is particularly valuable at this time, but we adults need to do it too. And we need to do this type of thinking in front of the children.

Why?

How we act is what they will do. Model creativity. Model exploring the arts, model going into nature, and model engaging in new experiences and with different types of people. Model a life of celebrating our brains, our minds, and the endless possibilities of our creativity.

Conclusion:

Your brain is dynamic. When you weave it with your mind, your soul, and your spirit, it will have endless adventures of compassion and greatness. Once we fully realize the integrated role our brain, body, soul, and spirit play together to help us create this life, there is no stopping us. Knowing the power of our brain, and what we can do to develop it, will give us the ability to not only function but to thrive in this highly complex and unknown environment.

Your brain is changeable. Your brain is intelligent. Your brain is beautiful.

Genein, Shawn, and Shayne Letford

'Create and Grow' Podcast
By Genein Letford

Episodes on Neuroscience and Creativity

- How Neuroscience Is Informing Leadership, DE&I and Intercultural Creativity for this New Era
  – Dr. Michael Platt, Episode #66

- The Neuroscience of Education: How to Empower Our Students by Teaching with the Brain in Mind
  - Dr. Kieran O'Mahoney, Episode #96

- The Business of Your Brain: How Neuroscience Gives Us Insight In Decisions and Imagination
  – Dr. Moran Serf, Episode #79

- The Neuroscience of Mindfulness, Meditation, and the Power of the Creative Brain
  – Dr. Nicole Tetreault, Episode #99

- The Neuroscience of Our Health, Our Arts and Our Freedom Ride
  - Dr. Peter Sterling, Episode #90

www.CAFFEstrategies.com/podcast

References

Why would musical training benefit the neural encoding of speech? The OPERA Hypothesis, Aniruddh D. Patel, 2011 Department of Theoretical Neurobiology, The Neuroscience Institute, San Diego, CA

Multiple Intelligences in Teaching and Education: Lessons Learned from Neuroscience, Shearer, Branton, Journal of Intelligence, 2018

Perception is Not Only a Matter of Now: Our Past Influences What We See, Donato Ramani, SISSA, Neuroscience News, May 16th, 2023

The Leader's Brain, Dr. Michael Platt, Wharton Press, 2020

Tomorrowmind, Dr. Kellerman and Dr. Martin Seligman, Artia Books, 2023

Social: How Our Brains are Wired to Connect, Dr. Matthew Lieberman, Crown, 2014

Your Brain on Art: How the Arts Transform Us, Dr. Susan Magsamen, Dr. Ivy Ross, Random House, 2023

Brain-centric Design: The Surprising Neuroscience Behind Learning with Deep Understanding, Rich Carr BcID and Dr. Kieran O'Mahony FRGS, 2018

The Brain With Dr. David Eagleman, PBS.org, 2015

My Love Affair with the Brain: The Life and Science of Dr. Marian Diamond, Documentary, Luna Productions, 2017

Praise for My Brain, My Brain, My Beautiful Brain

"My Brain My Brain My Beautiful Brain is insightful, heartfelt and inspires the reader to embrace their beautiful mind! The pearls of wisdom light up the pages and take the reader on an inner journey of exploring the strengths of their unique brain. A must read for children, families and educators seeking to explore the multicultural creativity of their mind."

-Nicole A. Tetreault, PhD Neuroscientist and Author of Insight into a Bright Mind

Shawn the Creative Kid is at it again! This time helping us to understand our creative brain. This is a great resource for teachers, parents, students, managers, and CEOs. If you are a Ph.D. in brain science, you already know this. If you are not, this book will help you to better understand what parts of the brain are firing when you are active in different arenas in your life! Use them all to be more creative! Great job, Shawn and Team Letford!

-Geoff McLachlan | Professionals at Play
Founder/CEO

"I love this book! It's a delightful way for kids- and adults- to understand the power and beauty of their creative brain."

-Natalie Nixon, PhD, CEO at Figure 8 Thinking, LLC

Partial proceeds from this book will support creative projects on Donorschoose.org. Visit Donorschoose.org to support a classroom today.

Genein M. Letford, M.Ed

As the 2019 LA Lakers Business Woman and the 2015 CA Charter Teacher of the Year, Genein is a national thought leader and creator of the concept of 'Intercultural Creativity® and NeuroSomatic Creativity®'. She is the Founder and Chief Creative Officer of CAFFE Strategies, INC which is a consulting, coaching, and training company that trains C-Suite executives, school leaders, and employees to create sustainable organizational equity and inclusion strategies, based on neuroscience, while unleashing their innovative thinking for themselves and in their businesses and schools.

Her *7 Gems of Intercultural Creativity®* is a leading framework that encourages corporations, healthcare systems and schools in their diversity and inclusion development while developing critical cognitive tools for creative thinking. Her first book, *From Debt To Destiny: Creating Financial Freedom From the Inside Out* connects creative thinking to financial agility and was an international bestseller in 5 finance categories. Her second book, *7 Gems of Intercultural Creativity: Connecting, Creating and Innovating Across Cultural Lines*, is the only book on this topic. She published her first children's book, *I AM CREATIVE!* with her 3-year-old son, Shawn Letford and is presenting her next leadership book, *Your Brain, Your Bias and the Beauty of Your Creative Mind* in early 2024. Genein believes creative thinking thrives best in an inclusive environment, and she is often called 'America's Creative Coach' for her work in reigniting intercultural creativity within our workforce. Genein lives in Arizona with her creative family.

@GeneinLetford

Shawn 'The Creative Kid' Letford

Shawn published his first book, *I AM CREATIVE*, at three years old and is on a mission to help the world 'Be More Creative'. He goes through his daily life giving his parents pure examples of creative thinking and inventive associations. He still enjoys sprinklers but has sparked an interest in flying drones and engineering. He loves being observant and plays his piano to exercise his mind. He'll be taking the stage to share about creative thinking and would love to visit your school or organization! As a five year old, a non-fiction book about sprinklers or drones will be his next literary project.

LinkedIn: Shawn the Creative Kid
IG: Creativekid_SL
Facebook:@creativeKidSL
Twitter:@Creativekid_SL

ABOUT THE AUTHORS

Shayne Letford

With a degree in Computer Science, Shayne Letford began his design career in 2009 when he started the company Letford Media. Letford Media has worked with many companies and business owners, coast to coast, developing amazing visual branding materials, which in turn increased their customer visibility and interaction. Shayne co-illustrated his first children's book, *I Am Creative* and now partnered with Briefstock to co-illustrate *My Brain My Brain, My Beautiful Brain*. Shayne is the Director of Technology and Branding for CAFFE Strategies, INC.

@LetfordMedia

Other Books

By The Authors

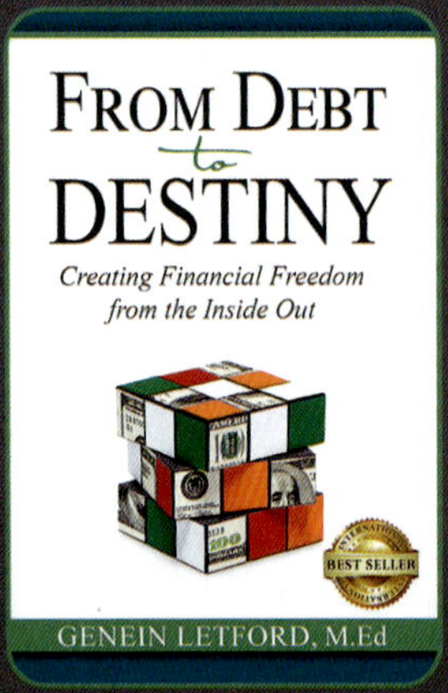

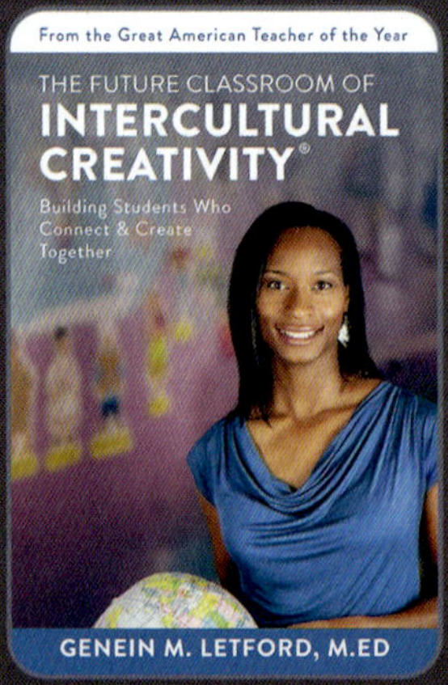

For more information, visit www.CAFFEstrategies.com

Professional Development for Companies, Organizations, and School Districts

PRISMATIC LEADERSHIP® SERIES

Power, Position and Purpose: Understanding Power Dynamics While Building Inclusive Teams

Prismatic Leadership® is complex. Brain research shows that authoritative power can inhibit leaders from seeing the plight of others. This power can lower their ability for connection, creativity and cultural awareness. Since creativity needs psychological safety, intellectual humility, curiosity and empathy to flourish, effective leaders must be aware of how power, position and authority can skew their perspective. Learn brain-based strategies to mitigate the effects of power and become an efficient Prismatic Leader®.

The Neuroscience of Leadership: Building A Culture of Trust in Diverse Teams

The science is clear: Trust is the new driver of productivity. Communicating your message, lowering fears (both rational and irrational), and pulling out the best of your team members requires strong Prismatic Leadership® skills. Scientists have identified the brain mechanisms that support our ability to connect and communicate with others, revealing how we can activate and strengthen them. Learn how to develop team chemistry and trust by building team identity through shared goals, values and social connection.

Empathetic Leadership: Building Cultural Sensitivity and Curiosity

Emotions lead, productivity follows; at least in the brain. Having a strong emotional foundation and understanding of the neuroscience behind how emotions work is an important aspect of emotional intelligence. Leaders will increase their emotional granularity (how to identify their emotions) and regulation. They will learn how to use these identifications for Intercultural Creativity® and leadership. This training uses interactive and reflective exercises for deep transformational learning in areas such as perspective shifting, curiosity development, vulnerability and empathy.

Reflective Leadership: Improve Self-Awareness, Resilience & Authenticity

Being able to understand yourself in uncertain times is an integral part of understanding and leading others. Improving brain based reflective practices that develop self-awareness, agile resilience and authenticity is now your most critical skill in this uncertain landscape. Prismatic Leaders will learn and implement the 5 elements of a resilient mindset and practice how to exercise these skills in various work experiences.

Intercultural Creativity® for Educators

In times like these, educators need to be culturally sensitive and creative with their lessons and their engagement strategies with students. Teaching diverse students calls for engaging brain centric designed curriculum. Recognizing that culturally responsive instruction helps educators close achievement gaps, CAFFE Strategies offers programs that expands the capacity of educators to serve students from diverse cultural and ethnic backgrounds while increasing creativity at the same time.

Three-Hour Interactive Session – Challenges educators to critically examine and strengthen their own instructional practices through a series of activities that teach participants how to become culturally competent educators by using culturally relevant curricula, employing culturally responsive teaching practices, facilitating school-wide cultural responsiveness, and forming professional learning communities.

NeuroSomatic Creativity® in the Classroom

To think creativity is only about the arts is wrong but to think one can reach their full creative potential without the arts is also incorrect. The creative arts (visual arts, dance, theatre and music) are integral parts of the human learning experience. Our unique NeuroSomatic Creativity® training guides educators through effective methods for integrating the creative arts within an established curriculum for increased engagement and exploration of the content.

This training specializes in connecting the neuroscience of the arts to metaphorical thinking, sensory observation, abstraction and more! Genein Letford has successfully lectured on arts integration at the university level and is pleased to bring her specialized program to educators across the nation. Let's get our students moving, painting, playing, creating and learning through the arts!

Certification programs are available. Visit CAFFEstrategies.com for more information.